W9-CNH-823

The Mackenzie River

by Tim Harris

Gareth Stevens Publishing
A WORLD ALMANAC EDUCATION GROUP COMPANY

Please visit our web site at: www.garethstevens.com
For a free color catalog describing Gareth Stevens Publishing's list of high-quality books and multimedia programs, call 1-800-542-2595 (USA) or 1-800-387-3178 (Canada). Gareth Stevens Publishing's fax: (414) 332-3567.

Library of Congress Cataloging-in-Publication Data

Harris, Tim.
The Mackenzie River / by Tim Harris.
p. cm. — (Rivers of North America)
Includes bibliographical references and index.
Contents: From source to mouth—The life of the river—Northern people—Land of black gold—Places to visit—How rivers form.
ISBN 0-8368-3756-8 (lib. bdg.)
1. Mackenzie River (N.W.T.)—Juvenile literature. [1. Mackenzie River (N.W.T.).]
I. Title. II. Series.
F1100.M3H37 2003
971.9'3—dc21 2003042741

This North American edition first published in 2004 by
Gareth Stevens Publishing
A World Almanac Education Group Company
330 West Olive Street, Suite 100
Milwaukee, Wisconsin 53212 USA

Author: Tim Harris
Editor: Tom Jackson
Consultant: Judy Wheatley Maben, Education Director, Water Education Foundation
Designer: Steve Wilson
Cartographer: Mark Walker
Picture Researcher: Clare Newman
Indexer: Kay Ollerenshaw
Managing Editor: Bridget Giles
Art Director: Dave Goodman

Gareth Stevens Editor: Betsy Rasmussen
Gareth Stevens Designer: Melissa Valuch

Picture Credits: Cover: Aklavik, Northwestern Territories on the banks of the Mackenzie River in winter. (Corbis: Lowell Georgia)
Contents: Yellowknife, Northwest Territories, Canada.

Key: l–left, r–right, t–top, b–bottom.
Ardea: M. Watson 15; Canadian Tourism Commission: 4, 8/9, 25, 26, 28, 29r, 29l; Corbis: Bettmann 27; Natalie Fobes 23; Lowell Georgia 5t, 22, 24; Historical Picture Archives 21r; Arthur Morris 11t; Galen Rowell 9b; Glenbow Archives: 5b, 16/17, 17r, 18 19, 20/21; NASA: Jacques Descloitres, MODIS Land Rapid Response Team, GSFC 8t; NHPA: Rich Kirchner 10; John Shaw 11b, 13; Still Pictures: Kim Heacox 14; Peter Arnold/S. J. Krasemann 12; Peter Arnold/Jim Wark 7

Printed in the United States of America

1 2 3 4 5 6 7 8 9 07 06 05 04 03

Table of Contents

River of the North

The Mackenzie River is a remote Canadian river. It flows through some of the coldest parts of the world and freezes over every year in winter, when it is dark for days on end.

The Mackenzie is an unusual river. For most of its length, it flows through an enormous evergreen forest that stretches either side for hundreds of miles (kilometers). It gets so cold in winter that the river freezes over. The ice becomes thick enough for people to drive on.

Ice River

The Mackenzie River is the third-longest river in North America, after the Missouri and Mississippi. It is also one of the most remote rivers anywhere in the world. Only a few small towns lie on its shores, and unlike other large rivers, most people live and work nearer to the river's source than where it flows into the sea. Usually, the area near a river's mouth is a busy place, but the Mackenzie's mouth at the Arctic Ocean is very different. It is a bitterly cold, icy wasteland where even the sea is frozen and the Sun does not rise for months on end.

The river itself freezes between November and June, and it flows over a layer of soil and rock that is always frozen solid. This permanently frozen layer is called the permafrost.

In Yellowknife, a town on Great Slave Lake where the Mackenzie River starts, the temperature in January is about –18°F (–28°C), but in July, the temperature is a much more pleasant 61°F (16°C)—almost as warm as Seattle, Washington, located much farther south. In winter, cold is not the only problem for people living near the Mackenzie. Since much of its course is north of the Arctic Circle, it remains dark all day in midwinter, and in summer, it remains light—even at night.

River People

Inuit and Dene people first made their homes close to the Mackenzie thousands of years ago, but the river is named for Scottish explorer Sir Alexander Mackenzie, the first European to follow its course from Great Slave Lake to the sea in 1789.

The Mackenzie's modern population is small because the river is so far away from other places. Only one road tracks the length of the river, and it is not open throughout the entire year. The Mackenzie River does attract visitors in summer, however, including a steady trickle of canoeists paddling downstream.

Above right: *The Mackenzie River winds through summer marshlands near its mouth. In winter, the marshes and the river freeze solid.*

Right: *An Inuit man crawls out of an igloo made from ice blocks near the mouth of the Mackenzie. Igloos are temporary shelters used during hunting trips.*

Left: *The city of Yellowknife on the shore of Great Slave Lake near the source of the river is the largest settlement in the region.*

1 From Source to Mouth

The Mackenzie River is the longest river in Canada. It flows northward to the icy Arctic Ocean through hundreds of miles of forested wilderness and frozen tundra.

The Mackenzie River flows 1,062 miles (1,770 km) from Great Slave Lake in Canada's Northwest Territories to the Beaufort Sea in the Arctic Ocean. The river drains about 681,000 square miles (1,765,000 sq km), nearly one-fifth of Canada.

Above: *Water thunders through the S-shaped Virginia Falls on the Nahanni River in the Northwest Territories.*

Great Lakes

Great Slave Lake is the world's tenth-largest and sixth-deepest lake. Because it is very deep, its waters remain cold throughout the year, and for at least six months every year, it freezes over. Great Slave Lake is named for the Slavey band of the Dene people, who have lived along its shores for thousands of years. The lake itself is fed by two other large rivers—the Hay and the Slave. The Slave supplies much of the Mackenzie's water, and it is an unusual river because it connects the Great Slave Lake to Lake Athabasca in Alberta. Lake Athabasca is fed by the Peace and Athabasca Rivers, which flow from the Rocky Mountains.

Yellowknife is on the northern shore of Great Slave Lake. It is the only city in the Mackenzie Valley and has a population of just 17,500 people.

KEY FACTS

Length:	1,062 miles (1,770 km)
Drainage basin:	681,000 square miles (1,765,000 square kilometers)
Source:	Great Slave Lake
Mouth:	Mackenzie Delta, Beaufort Sea
Natural features:	Great Bear Lake, The Ramparts, Mackenzie Delta
Economic uses:	Transportation, fishing, oil and gas exploration
Major settlements:	Yellowknife, Fort Providence, Fort Simpson, Norman Wells, Fort Good Hope, Inuvik

Mountain Water

The Mackenzie River flows out of the west end of Great Slave Lake, near Fort Providence, which is a small Native community on a high bank overlooking the river.

At Fort Simpson, the waters of the Liard River flow into the Mackenzie. Floatplanes take off from the river here to take people to remoter destinations. The town was first built as a fur-trading post and was originally called Fort of the Forks. The Liard River flows from high in the Canadian Rockies, merging with the waters of the Nahanni River on its way. The Nahanni tumbles down from the rugged Mackenzie Mountains and is popular with enthusiasts of water sports because of its rapids. Its largest waterfall—Virginia Falls—is twice as high as Niagara Falls.

River Road

West of Fort Simpson, the Mackenzie is as large as 2 miles (3 km) wide in some places. A road follows the river for more than one hundred miles to Wrigley, where the road ends. In winter, cars can drive on the frozen river as far as Fort Good Hope on the edge of the Arctic Circle. Opposite Wrigley, a sheer cliff rises almost vertically 1,300 feet (400 meters) above the river.

The Mackenzie River flows almost due north between Wrigley and Tulita. In the Dene language, *Tulita* means "where two rivers meet." It is where the Mackenzie is joined by the Great Bear River. The Great Bear runs just 77 miles (128 km) from Great Bear Lake. While not as deep as Great Slave Lake, Great Bear Lake covers an even greater area.

The Mackenzie River swings northwest near Tulita and flows toward Norman Wells, an old oil town. Six artificial islands were built in the river so drilling could continue after the river had thawed.

Above: *A satellite image showing the Mackenzie Delta. The water of Mackenzie Bay is turned brown by the mud washed out to sea by the river.*

To the Arctic

The Mackenzie River runs a straighter course than many rivers, but near Fort Good Hope, there is a big S-bend as it first swings to the northeast, then back to the

Main Image: *The Sun dips below the horizon across the wide Mackenzie River. The river is too wide for bridges to be built across it.*

northwest. After Fort Good Hope was established as a trading post in 1805, it attracted Dene and Inuit people. Just upstream of the town are The Ramparts, where 650-foot (200-m) cliffs force the river through a spectacular, narrow canyon.

Marshy Delta

As it approaches the sea, the single channel of the river breaks into several channels, separated by islands and marshy areas. This area is called the Mackenzie Delta. Before 1961, the capital of the delta, and the Mackenzie's most northerly town, was Aklavik. Each spring when the ice broke up, the town flooded, and in 1954, the Canadian government decided to construct a new town in a safer place. So Inuvik was created a few miles south on the east side of the delta. Inuvik is the major transportation center in the Mackenzie Delta, with regular flights to Yellowknife and other Canadian towns. Inuvik is also a center for oil and gas exploration.

North of Inuvik, the trees thin out and become shorter, as forest is replaced by bare tundra. The tundra is inhabited by Inuit people. The Inuit live in small communities along the coast of the Arctic Ocean.

Below: *The Great Slave Lake, where the Mackenzie River gets most of its water.*

2 The Life of the River

The wildlife living near the Mackenzie River has to survive in extreme environments. The winters are very cold and dark, and in summer, flooding is common after the ice melts.

For most of its length, the Mackenzie River meanders through the vast forests that stretch across Canada from the Pacific to the Atlantic coasts. It is a type of forest called taiga, which is a mix of mostly evergreen trees, such as black spruce, larch, jack pine, and aspen. These trees have waxy, needlelike leaves that can withstand the region's harsh winters, when temperatures remain below freezing for months on end.

The trees grow slowly, and in the far north, the trees grow only a few feet tall. The taiga is broken in places by boggy marshes and lakes.

Toward its delta, the Mackenzie River leaves the forest and flows through barren tundra. Trees are rare in the tundra, but grasses or low-growing shrubs survive here.

Left: *An American black bear climbs a pine tree. Black bears are expert climbers. They use their long claws to grab branches.*

BISON AND CRANES

Just south of Great Slave Lake, Wood Buffalo National Park was created to protect fifteen hundred wood bison. This number was later boosted by the introduction of several thousand plains bison from Alberta. Unfortunately, the new arrivals brought diseases with them. Many bison had to be slaughtered, but their numbers in the refuge are now steady at about three thousand. The national park also provides a home for beavers, muskrat, moose, lynx, wolves, and black bears.

The park's rarest and most famous residents are whooping cranes (right), birds that spend winter months to the south in Texas. In the 1950s, the world population of whooping cranes was fewer than fifty, but the protection given them in Wood Buffalo National Park has helped increase their numbers to almost two hundred.

Staying Alive

Animals survive the winter cold along the Mackenzie River in a variety of ways. Some migrate (travel long distances) to places where there is more food, returning again the following spring. Others change their eating habits during the winter months. Still others stay alive by hibernating—going into a long, sleeplike state.

Wood frogs feed in the river during the summer, but in winter, they are frozen alive as the river ices over. The frogs survive, however, and become active again after the ice melts in spring.

River Fish

Millions of fish live in the Mackenzie River for at least part of the year, including Arctic grayling, Arctic lamprey, lake trout, lake whitefish, pickerel, and inconnu. The inconnu is one of the river's largest fish, with the heaviest specimen ever caught weighing

Below: *A female spruce grouse perches on a pine tree. Male spruce grouse have more colorful feathers than the females, which they use to attract mates.*

63 pounds (29 kilograms). Named *poisson inconnu* (meaning "unknown fish") by French explorers, this fish has a broad head and thrives in the river and nearby lakes. In the fall, inconnu swim down the river and out to sea. Some adult fish return to the river in spring to breed. The inconnu living in Great Slave Lake do not migrate to the sea but remain in the lake all their lives.

On the Bank

The Mackenzie's fish provide a rich source of food for some birds and other animals—but only during the warm, summer months. River otters, bald eagles, ospreys, belted kingfishers, wolverines, and black bears are some of those that prey on fish. However, when the river is frozen during the winter, these fish eaters cannot get through the ice to the fish beneath. Animals

FLOWERS IN THE TUNDRA

The tundra is a cold environment for most of the year, much too cold for most plants to grow. However, during the short summer—just sixty or seventy days every year—the Sun never sets. The hardy plants that have survived the frosts and snow take full advantage of the twenty-four-hour daylight. More than one hundred species of wild flowers, such as cotton grass (below), grow on the islands of the Mackenzie Delta. The brightly colored flowers attract the insects that thrive in the marshy land. Birds travel thousands of miles to the tundra in summer to feed on the insects and flower seeds.

that eat river fish have to switch to other foods or travel to areas where fish are available all year-round. Ospreys, kingfishers, and bald eagles fly south or west to the unfrozen shores of the Pacific Ocean, while river otters hunt small land animals. The river's banks provide breeding sites in summer for shorebirds and Arctic terns. These birds migrate thousands of miles south when the water freezes.

Forest Hunters

The forests on either side of the river are home to a variety of hunting animals. Wolves, wolverines, coyotes, bobcats, and lynx hunt other animals or feed on the dead bodies of animals.

Black bears are meat eaters, but they also eat fruits and berries. Black bears do not hibernate during the whole winter but go into a deep sleep during just the coldest periods. This helps them cut

Left: *A goshawk keeps a look-out for prey from a perch high in a pine tree.*

down on the amount of food they need when food is hard to find. Black bears live in forests, but white polar bears hunt in tundra regions and on the sea ice around the Mackenzie Delta. They prey on seals, birds, and fish.

Bird Life

Some birds are predators, too. The goshawk builds its nest in large forest trees and ambushes other birds. Unlike the goshawk, the great gray owl is a nocturnal hunter. It hunts at night for mice and other rodents. Most of the birds that live along the Mackenzie River during the summer feed on huge swarms of insects. Without the insects, these birds would starve, and since insects are active only when the weather is warm, the birds have to fly south during the fall, returning again the next spring. Some birds, however, stay for the winter. Spruce grouse feed on berries and pine needles; crossbills gouge seeds from cones; and woodpeckers are able to chisel deep into tree bark to find grubs.

Plant Eaters

Birds are not the only animals to migrate. During the fall, huge herds of caribou gather

Below: *A herd of caribou runs across a shallow stream while grazing on the tundra during summer.*

THE SECRETIVE GLUTTON

Wolverines have earned a reputation as fierce hunters, and a 45-pound (20-kg) adult is quite capable of chasing and killing a caribou. Mostly, however, these secretive meat eaters prey upon smaller land animals, fish, or carrion (dead animals)—often the abandoned meal of a wolf pack. Wolverines use their powerful jaws and sharp teeth to crush and tear the flesh of prey, even when it is frozen. Wolverines are able to survive the bitter cold winter in the Mackenzie River Valley, and they do not hibernate. Their wide paws act like snowshoes, preventing the animals from sinking in deep snow, while a thick coat of brown and black fur provides insulation against the cold.

Above: *Wolverines are relatives of weasels.*

on the tundra and travel west to the forests beside the Mackenzie River, where they eat leaves and bark. They return to the tundra the following spring to graze on the grass and moss growing there.

Other plant eaters that live close to the Mackenzie include wood bison, moose, musk oxen, and elk (also known as wapiti). Moose sometimes come to the shores of the Mackenzie to drink and to eat water plants growing in the shallows. They are the world's largest deer. Adult males stand more than 6 feet (1.8 m) high and have large, forked antlers. Moose have very long legs, which help them wade through deep winter snow and step over large fallen logs in the forest.

3 Northern People

The first people to live beside the Mackenzie River led difficult lives. They survived by hunting animals in summer before settling in for the long, cold winter.

The first people to live beside the Mackenzie River probably came to the area from Siberia in Asia about 35,000 years ago. Some experts believe they traveled across a strip of land that connected Siberia with Alaska until 12,000 years ago. The Dene people who still live by the river are related to these first arrivals. At that time, the weather was much colder than it is now, because a massive ice sheet covered much of Canada. About 4,500 years ago, weather conditions became milder, the ice retreated, and thick forests grew up around the Mackenzie River.

Tough Life

A later wave of migrants probably crossed the Bering Strait in dugout canoes. These newcomers were the ancestors of the Inuit,

Below: *A Dene woman and her dog at the door of a tepee at the end of the nineteenth century. These tents were used for shelter in summer.*

who live in the most northerly parts of Canada, including near the mouth of the Mackenzie River.

Even after the weather got warmer, life was still very difficult for the inhabitants of the region. The land was forested and rocky, making it impossible to grow food, so the people who lived along the Mackenzie had to hunt the animals that lived there. They became very skilled at tracking and killing moose and caribou.

There were at least seven different bands of Dene people: the Chipewyan, Dogrib, Gwich'in, Hare, Loucheux, Nahanni, and Slavey. They were nomadic people, frequently moving from place to place while hunting and gathering fruits.

TRADITIONAL LIFESTYLE

Dene people used nets made from caribou sinews to catch fish from the Mackenzie River and trap small mammals along its banks. They hunted larger animals with bows and arrows and killed beavers with clubs. Women and children collected strawberries, raspberries, and rose hips, carrying them in bark baskets. Much of the Dene's clothing was crafted from moose hides and beaver fur.

The Dene used to be nomadic people. During the warmer months of the year, they lived in cone-shaped tents made from wood poles covered with moose hides or bark. During the bitter winter months, they sheltered in low log cabins, with the gaps between the logs plugged with moss and clay. Each cabin had a smoke hole in a pitched roof that was covered with spruce boughs. Traditionally, the Dene lived in small family groups of about twenty men, women, and children.

Above: *A Dene woman belonging to the Slavey band shows off a caribou hide at the beginning of the twentieth century. Hides were used to make tepees and clothes.*

Some of the Dene bands, such as the Slavey, stayed close to the Mackenzie River because it provided plenty of fish in summer months and was a useful travel route.

The Inuit settled around the Mackenzie Delta and at other places along the Arctic Coast, hunting seals and bowhead whales in the spring and moving inland to kill caribou in the summer. In the fall, the Inuit prepared for the winter by storing food that would keep them alive during the cold, dark months when they would not be able to hunt.

Trade Mission

Things started to change dramatically in the mid-eighteenth century. Cree people from the east met visiting Europeans and acquired many new things, such as tobacco, sugar, and guns. When groups of Cree came into contact with the Dene, they began trading these products with them, and this attracted European businesspeople to the area.

In 1789, the Scottish businessman and explorer Alexander Mackenzie was the first European to travel the entire length of the river that eventually received his name. One of the reasons for his journey was to check whether there were any Native people along the river with whom to trade. He also wanted to see if the river could be used as a route to the Pacific Ocean. After discovering the river flowed into the Arctic Ocean

Above: *An early picture of Yellowknife on the shore of the Great Slave Lake. Yellowknife grew up as a mining center.*

A MAN WITH A MISSION

In June 1789, Alexander Mackenzie (right) set out with a small group of Europeans and a party of Chipewyan Denes to travel what is now the Mackenzie River. Their three canoes were stacked with beads, mirrors, knives, and other goods. After paddling to the mouth of the river, they turned around and paddled back again, the whole trip taking 102 days. They traded with Native people along the way, swapping their cargo for beaver furs. They also encouraged people to bring their furs to a trading post on the shores of Lake Athabasca. Mackenzie was discouraged that the river had not led to the Pacific Ocean and initially called it the "River of Disappointment." Mackenzie was a careful observer of everything around him, and among his sightings was the presence of oil at the place now called Norman Wells. He had no idea, however, how important oil was to become.

and not the Pacific, Mackenzie traveled south again before the river froze over.

The First Towns

The first trading post was established on the river in 1796 at Livingston's Fort. Over the next eighty years, several more were founded at Fort Simpson, Fort Good Hope, Fort McPherson, and other places. The Dene were encouraged to bring furs and other goods to the trading posts, where they were exchanged for rifles, clothing, tea, and tobacco. These items were brought into the area by two British companies: the Hudson's Bay Company and the North West Company—Alexander Mackenzie was a partner in this company. Eventually, all these trading posts became permanent towns, and some of them still survive today.

In the nineteenth century, the territory containing the Mackenzie River was run by the Hudson's Bay Company. In 1869, the Canadian government paid £300,000 ($450,000) to buy most of the company's lands. Twenty years later, it was discovered that the Mackenzie River area was rich in precious metals and oil, and the government decided to take some of the land away from the Native people.

When European trappers and gold prospectors moved into the area, conflict grew between them and the Dene. A treaty was signed in 1921 to ease the tensions. The Native bands, members of the Dene Nation, lost their titles to traditional lands but kept the right to use the land for hunting. They also received small cash payments, free schooling, farm tools, and guarantees to some of the land.

AKAITCHO, A FRIEND TO TRADERS

One of the Native bands that lived around the Great Slave Lake was the Yellowknife people. Their greatest leader was Akaitcho (below), who led the tribe when it was at its strongest in the 1820s and 1830s. Akaitcho was friendly with European traders and explorers, and he helped the British adventurer John Franklin on his expedition to the Arctic. Between 1819 and 1822, Akaitcho and other Yellowknife guided Franklin as he looked for a water route down the Mackenzie River to Asia. Franklin died later in the Arctic Ocean, but his exploration of the area would not have been possible at all without the help of Akaitcho. Most of the Yellowknife people died in an outbreak of influenza in 1928.

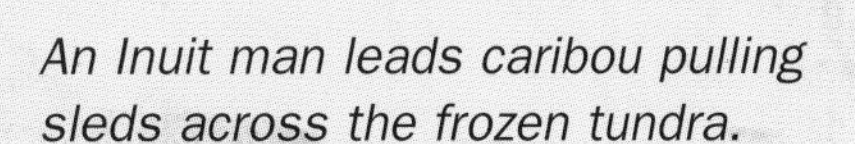

An Inuit man leads caribou pulling sleds across the frozen tundra.

4 Land of Black Gold

The Mackenzie River has many natural resources, from diamonds and gold to petroleum oil. Many people in the area work to extract and refine these minerals.

All the modern towns along the Mackenzie River were originally trading posts. Traders working for the Hudson's Bay Company and the North West Company brought products such as metal tools, guns, and tobacco down the river on boats to the posts. Native people came to the trading posts to exchange furs and hides for these products. Over the years, Native people began to settle at the posts, which eventually became permanent towns.

Oil Field

Norman Wells is the only town on the Mackenzie that did not begin in this way. The Dene people knew about the oil that seeped

Below: *Drilling ships are surrounded by ice as they search for oil in the Arctic Ocean near the mouth of the Mackenzie River.*

GOLDEN HOPES

Yellowknife, situated on Great Slave Lake in the Northwest Territories, is the most northerly city in Canada. More than half the people who live near the Mackenzie River live in Yellowknife. Named for the copper knives the local Native people used, Yellowknife did not prosper until gold seekers started digging in the area in the 1930s. Very few of the newcomers struck it rich, but people kept coming in the hope of making a fortune.

Their city did not even have a road connecting it to other towns until 1967. Before then, visitors had to travel by barge or plane. Yellowknife now has government offices, an airfield, a hospital, and several gold mines, but still only 17,500 people live there.

from the riverbank there, and Alexander Mackenzie reported seeing it during his expedition in 1789. The first oil wells, however, were not drilled there until 1919. Soon the town was thriving, as powerful barges brought supplies up the river and took the oil away. At its peak, 160 wells near Norman Wells produced 420 million gallons (1.5 billion liters) of oil every year. Six artificial islands were built in the Mackenzie River so drilling could continue all year-round, not just when the river was frozen over. A refinery was built at

Above: *A large excavator digs up rocks and loads them onto huge dump trucks at a diamond mine near Yellowknife.*

THE MAD TRAPPER

The economy of the Mackenzie River grew up around trapping animals for their furs. Trappers had to be hardy people, and many spent long periods alone. One trapper was a mysterious man who called himself Albert Johnson. He arrived in Fort McPherson in 1931. Soon, people were complaining that their traps were being interfered with, and Constable King, a local mountie (mounted police officer), went to question Johnson. King was met with a hail of bullets, so he organized a seven-man posse from Aklavik to arrest the stranger. After a fifteen-hour siege, Johnson escaped and was pursued by mounties into the mountains in temperatures below –40°F (–40°C). He survived for seven weeks in terrible conditions before—surrounded by seventeen mounties—he was bombed from a plane. Johnson did not stand a chance, but no one ever discovered who he really was.

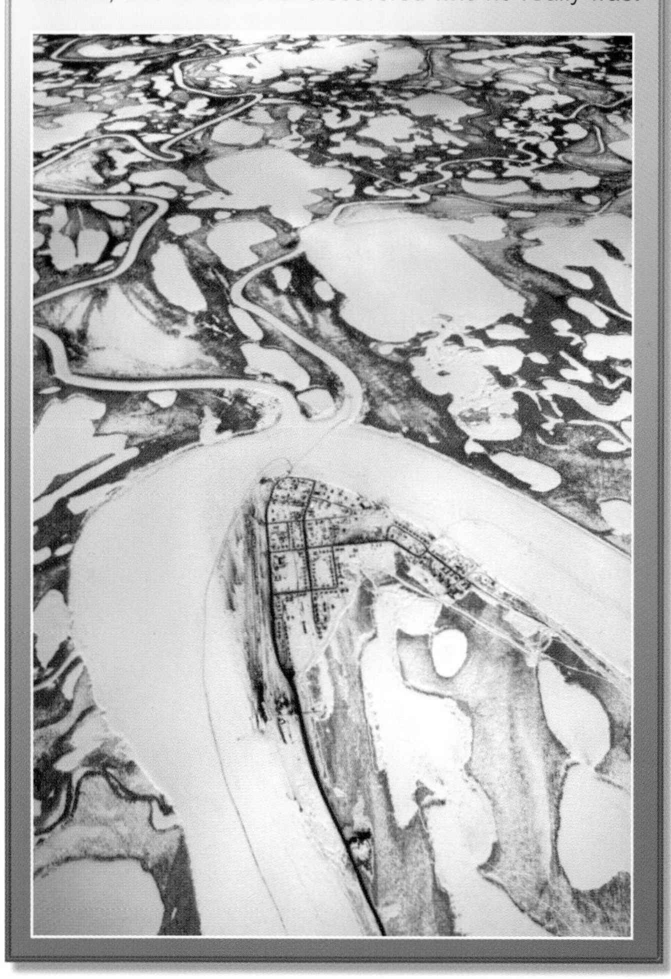

Norman Wells to turn the crude oil into valuable petroleum products.

Pipe Dream

During the 1970s, the Mackenzie River became busy as long convoys of barges carried drills, pipes, and other machinery down the river. Geologists had discovered that there was much more oil than had been thought, both under the river and in the Arctic Ocean, far to the north. However, this new oil would have to be carried in a long pipeline. The region's Native people did not want to have the pipeline running through their land, and the Canadian government agreed with them. Without the pipeline, Mackenzie's oil boom never happened. Several barge companies went out of business, and in 1996, the Norman Wells oil field itself was shut down.

Nevertheless, the Mackenzie River is still a busy cargo route. Barges traveling up and down the river between Yellowknife and towns near the mouth, such as Inuvik, are still a familiar sight during the summer months when the Mackenzie is not

Left: *The village of Aklavik on a bend in the Mackenzie River. Police set out from here to catch the mad trapper.*

frozen. When the river freezes over in fall, it becomes an ice road used by trucks and snow cats.

The Rush for Gold

While oil was known as "black gold," the Mackenzie Valley also had the real thing. Miners on their way to the Yukon Territory at the end of the nineteenth century were the first to discover gold at Yellowknife, but there was no big gold rush because the area was so isolated. In the 1930s, however, prospectors began to use floatplanes (small aircraft that can take off and land on water) to reach more remote spots, and hundreds of gold claims were staked. Very few people struck it rich, but a few gold, uranium, and diamond mines still operate in the area.

With the arrival of miners, Yellowknife expanded, but it was cut off from the outside world for much of the year, and so it never grew into more than a medium-sized town. The year 1967 was very important for the economy of the MacKenzie River because that was when an all-weather road was completed, linking Yellowknife to the outside cities of Hay River and Peace River in Alberta. People could now get to Yellowknife at any time. They were no longer dependent on light planes to access the town for much

Below: *Many of the Mackenzie's people, such as this Inuit man, enjoy leading a traditional way of life.*

Above: *One of the best ways to get around in the wilderness of the Mackenzie Valley is to fly. Floatplanes can take off and land on stretches of calm water.*

of the year. Once the road was built, Yellowknife was named the capital of the Northwest Territories, and many new office jobs were created. The government is the biggest employer in Yellowknife, but nearby mines also bring wealth to the city.

Fish Harvest

Fishing has always been important for the people who live in the Mackenzie Valley, and both the river and lakes are well stocked. Catching the fish, however, is a seasonal industry because the river and lakes are frozen for months.

In 1945, commercial fishing was established in the Great Slave Lake, and it soon became the town of Hay River's most important industry. The city's eight plants process as much as 10 million tons (9 million tonnes) of fish every year.

Wilderness Visitors

Tourism is now the biggest growth industry in the Mackenzie River region. Some visitors come to experience the solitude found in the wilderness landscapes of the national parks, while others seek firsthand views of the extraordinary wildlife.

LAND RITES VERSUS OIL

When the big petroleum companies discovered the large reserves of oil and gas under the MacKenzie River, they planned to build a pipeline along the valley to bring these valuable fossil fuels to southern Canada and the United States. Native people opposed the plan, fearing the construction work and the pipeline itself would interfere with the migration of the caribou herds, so vital for their way of life. In 1977, a special inquiry by Judge Thomas Berger ruled that the pipeline could only go ahead after the Native people's land claims had been settled, something which did not happen for another seven years. Today, no new oil field can be opened up in the region without the consent of the local people.

Many canoeists take the challenge and paddle the Mackenzie each summer, while thrill seekers ride the whitewater of the Nahanni River. Traditional Native craftspeople are kept busy making souvenirs for tourists. While tourism is becoming an important part of the river's economy, most local people earn a living as they always have—by trapping and fishing.

Above: *An oil pipeline at Inuvik near the mouth of the Mackenzie River.*

5 Places to Visit

More and more people visit the Mackenzie River every year to view the magnificent scenery, watch the wildlife, and learn about its Native American heritage.

1 Twin Falls Territorial Park, NT
This small park is named for the two waterfalls on the Hay River south of the Great Slave Lake. Alexandra Falls is higher than Louise Falls (right), which is a little way upstream. Hikers can get a good view of the falls from viewing platforms.

2 Hay River, NT
Situated on the south side of Great Slave Lake, this town of 3,600 residents is an important fishing port. Its eight fish factories process ten million tons (9 million tonnes) of whitefish every year. The airport at Hay River is busy with travelers arriving and departing in and out of the region.

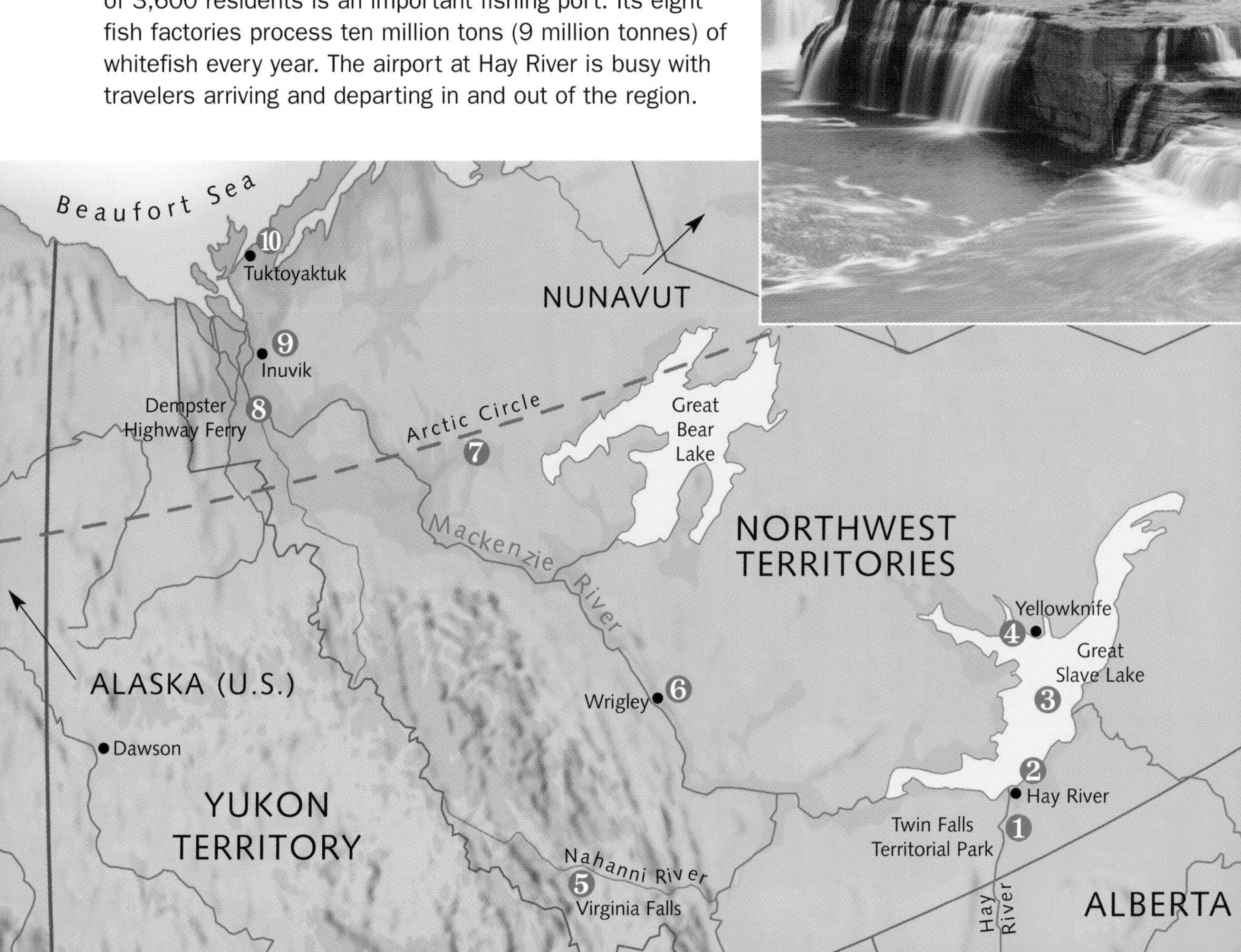

③ Great Slave Lake, NT
The waters of the Mackenzie River flow from this lake, which is frozen from November to June every year. Several large rivers feed the lake, the largest of which is the Slave River.

④ Yellowknife, NT
This city in the Mackenzie River area was named for the Yellowknife people, who moved into the area in the early 1800s. The oldest part of the town is on an island in Great Slave Lake. Yellowknife is sometimes called "Canada's biggest little town."

⑤ Virginia Falls, NT
On the South Nahanni River, Virginia Falls is twice the height of Niagara Falls. The river below the falls is a favorite place with whitewater enthusiasts.

⑥ Wrigley, NT
A traditional Dene community and home for about two hundred people who live in log cabins. The town is also called *Roche-qui-trempe-a-l'eau*—French for "rock which plunges into the water"—for the tall cliffs in the area.

⑦ Arctic Circle

The Arctic Circle is an imaginary line that rings the northern part of the globe. North of the Arctic Circle, the Sun never sets on at least one day each summer and does not rise for at least one day each winter. At the North Pole itself, the Sun stays up for an entire six months and sets for another six months.

Above: *The awesome glow of the Northern Lights can be seen on clear nights north of the Arctic Circle.*

⑧ Dempster Highway Ferry, NT
A road joins Inuvik with Dawson in the Yukon Territory. In winter, travelers can drive across the frozen Mackenzie River near Fort McPherson. In summer, however, they must use a ferry. Each fall, the ferry has to be hauled out of the icy river. While the river is freezing and thawing, nobody can get across.

⑨ Igloo Church, Inuvik, NT
The Our Lady of Victory Church in Inuvik is fondly known by another name—the Igloo Church. The church's dome (above) makes it look a little like an igloo—a round Inuit hunting lodge made from ice. The dome is a town landmark.

⑩ Tuktoyaktuk, NT
Tuktoyaktuk, or Tuk, is a small Inuit community on the coast of the Beaufort Sea, near the mouth of the Mackenzie River. The city is surrounded by pingos—huge ice-covered hills. Tuk is one of the few places where tourists can hunt polar bears by dog team.

How Rivers Form

Rivers have many features that are constantly changing in shape. The illustration below shows how these features are created.

Rivers flow from mountains to oceans, receiving water from rain, melting snow, and underground springs. Rivers collect their water from an area called the river basin. High mountain ridges form the divides between river basins.

Tributaries join the main river at places called confluences. Rivers flow down steep mountain slopes quickly but slow as they near the ocean and gather more water. Slow rivers have many meanders (wide turns) and often change course.

Near the mouth, levees (piles of mud) build up on the banks. The levees stop water from draining into the river, creating areas of swamp.

1. **Glacier:** An ice mass that melts into river water.
2. **Lake:** The source of many rivers; may be fed by springs or precipitation.
3. **Rapids:** Shallow water that flows quickly.
4. **Waterfall:** Formed when a river wears away softer rock, making a step in the riverbed.
5. **Canyon:** Formed when a river cuts a channel through rock.
6. **Floodplain:** A place where rivers often flood flat areas, depositing mud.
7. **Oxbow lake:** River bend cut off when a river changes course, leaving water behind.
8. **Estuary:** River mouth where river and ocean water mix together.
9. **Delta:** Triangular river mouth created when mud islands form, splitting the flow into several channels called distributaries.

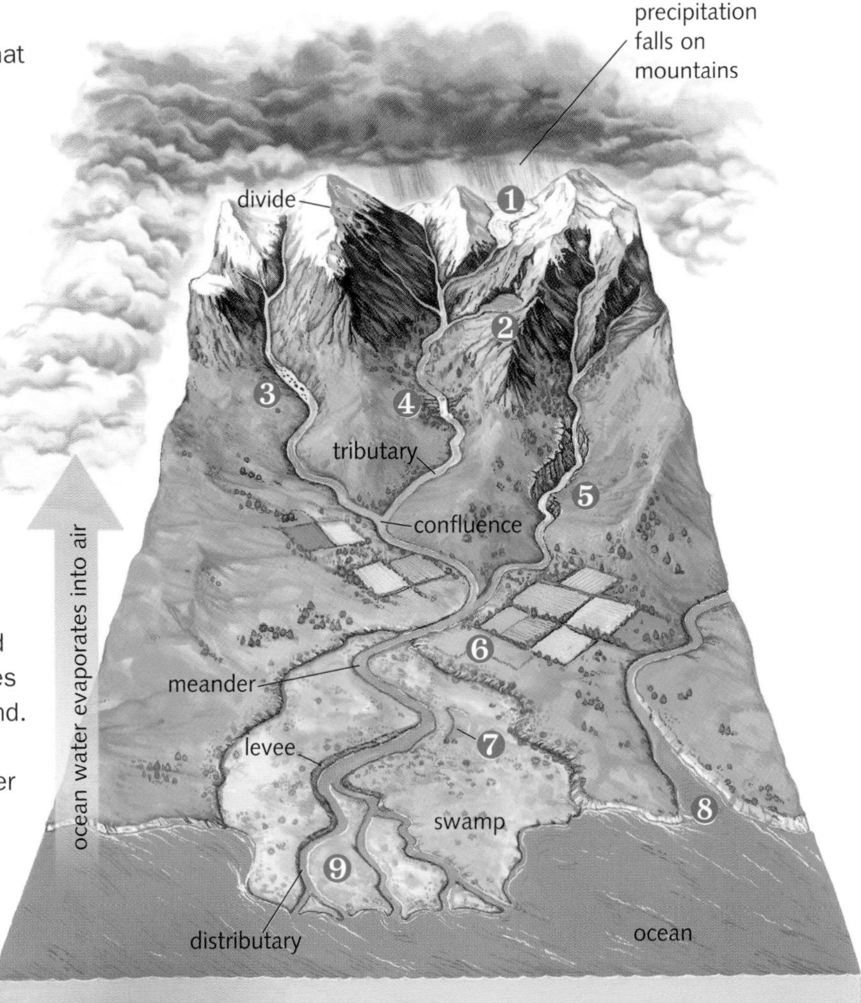

Glossary

Arctic The frigid area of the world that surrounds the North Pole.

artificial Made by people.

barge A flat-bottomed boat used to transport goods and usually pulled or pushed by a tug.

basin The area drained by a river and its tributaries.

cargo Transported products or merchandise.

confluence The place where rivers meet.

dam A constructed barrier across a river that controls the flow of water.

heritage Property, culture, or traditions inherited from previous generations.

industry Producing things or providing services in order to earn money.

inquiry An official investigation.

migration A regular journey undertaken by a group of animals from one climate to another for feeding and breeding purposes.

reservoir An artificial lake where water is stored for later use.

source The place where a river begins.

taiga A forest of conifer trees that grows in the cold, northern regions of the world.

tributary A river that flows into a larger river at a confluence.

tundra A plains area near the Arctic region that has a permanently frozen subsoil.

valley A hollow channel cut by a river usually between ranges of hills or mountains.

For Further Information

Books

Dabcovich, Lydia. *The Polar Bear Son: An Inuit Tale.* Clarion Books, 1999.

Levert, Suzanne. *Northwest Territories. Canada in the 21st Century* series. Chelsea House Publications, 2001.

Livesey, Robert. *Native Peoples.* Stoddart Kids, 1994.

Manson, Ainslie. *A Dog Came, Too.* Douglas & McIntyre Publishing Group, 2003.

Wallace, Mary. *The Inuksuk Book.* Owl Communications, 1999.

Web Sites

Canada's Aquatic Environment
www.aquatic.uoguelph.ca

Destination Arctic
www.destinationarctic.com/lore/cdn_arctic.shtml

The Mackenzie River
greatcanadianrivers.com/rivers/mack/mack-home.html

Virtual Guidebook to the Lower Mackenzie
www.virtualguidebooks.com/NWT/LowerMackenzie.html

Index

DISCARD